FAME and FAITH

Discipleship Ministry Team
Ministry Council
Cumberland Presbyterian
Church

November 2017

8207 Traditional Place
Cordova (Memphis), Tennessee 38016

MINISTRY COUNCIL
Cumberland Presbyterian Church

Copyright page:

Funded, in part, by your
contributions to Our United Outreach.

OUR UNITED OUTREACH
Made Possible In Part By Your Tithe To Our United Outreach

FAME and FAITH

WHAT MAKES A CELEBRITY?. 4
Our Culture's Obsession With Celebrity Is Not Spritually Healthy.

CHRISTIANS IN A CELEBRITY CULTURE: POP CULTURE CHRISTIANS 12
Observing Christians who live in celebrity culture can help teach us how to live faithfully in a celebrity–obsessed culture.

SURRENDERING CELEBRITY FOR THE SAVIOR'S SAKE: GIVING IT UP FOR GOD 18
An overview of the Presbyterian family of churches, with a brief comparison to the Cumberland Presbyterian Church.

USING CELEBRITY FOR CHRIST 24
Christian celebrities can reach many people for Christ, reminding us that all Christians are called to use their platforms to share the gospel with others.

BEHIND THE SCENES OF CELEBRITY. 32
Celebrities don't become celebrities all on their own. It takes a lot of people doing a lot of work to make the Church what it's supposed to be: the Body of Christ.

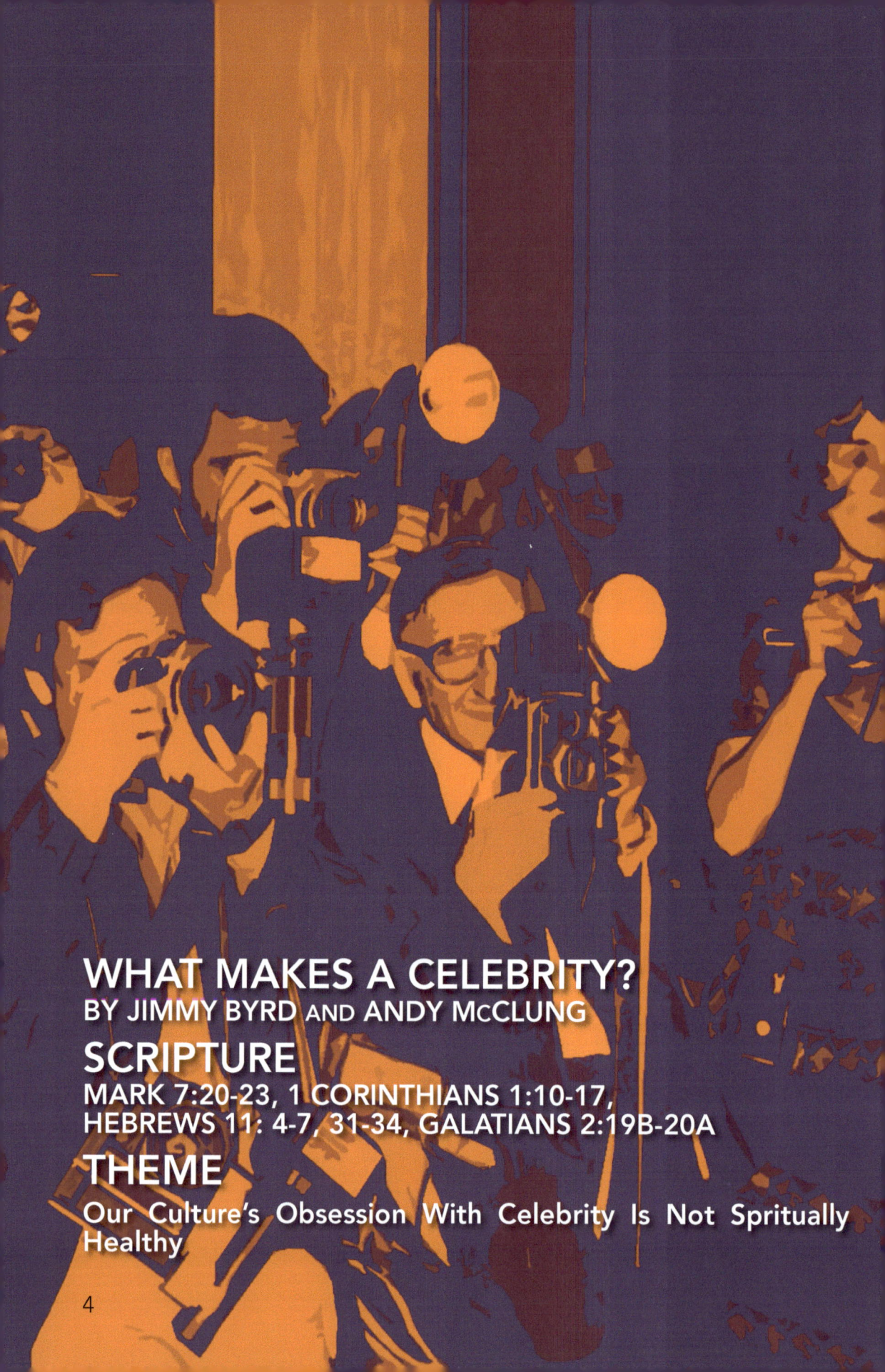

WHAT MAKES A CELEBRITY?
BY JIMMY BYRD AND ANDY McCLUNG

SCRIPTURE
MARK 7:20-23, 1 CORINTHIANS 1:10-17,
HEBREWS 11: 4-7, 31-34, GALATIANS 2:19B-20A

THEME
Our Culture's Obsession With Celebrity Is Not Spritually Healthy

🪙LEADER INSIGHT

Someone wrote to a teen advice website, "I want to be famous. I'm not sure what my talent is, but I really want to give it a try. Any tips?" The site's expert wisely said that most people working in fame-producing fields aren't famous; fame relies on lots of hard work and even more luck, and seeking fame (especially with no identified talent) will probably end in disappointment. This level-headed response, however, began by affirming the teen's unrealistic (but common) desire: I want to be famous.

While plenty of people have no desire for fame, most teens apparently do. A 2007 survey revealed the top (by far) two life goals for US young adults were to be rich and famous. Another 2007 study by UCLA showed pre-teens' top desire for their future was to be famous. A 2011 study by Christian Children's Fund reported that in developing countries, about half of 10 to 12 year olds want to enter helping professions (teachers, doctors), but in the western/developed countries, about half want to pursue fame as actors, singers, or fashion designers.

Talented or not, then, about half of your students hope to become celebrities.

EXPLAINING THE TOPIC

"Celebrity" comes from a Latin word meaning "often repeated"; it shares a root with "celebrate" and has been in the English language for 650 years.

It's not newsworthy that a cashier at your grocery store is getting divorced, or that a local school bus driver has an opinion on the environment. But when Brad and Jennifer got divorced and when Alec had something to say about the environment, it was all over the news. What's the difference? Celebrity.

Celebrities' actions and opinions are treated as worthy of our attention, even important enough for inclusion on the nightly news. Most people who don't know that cashier and bus driver don't really care what they do or say. Many people, however, don't consider celebrities strangers. They feel as if they know them, even though they've never met.

Some people might be curious about a stranger's life, but not enough to spend much time searching the web, reading magazines, or watching TV shows about them. In fact, if strangers shared with us the same details about their lives that we actively seek about celebrities' lives, we would probably run away.

There are different types of celebrities, but most are in entertainment: athletes, sports commentators, radio personalities, talk show hosts, actors, singers, dancers, directors, novelists, game show hosts. Non-entertainment folks can be celebrities too, such as news persons and political commentators. Some, politicians have celebrity status. There are people famous for being Christians—high-profile pastors, preachers, evangelists, teachers, and authors. Some people become celebrities because of the crimes they commit. There are even people who become famous without really doing anything. Maybe they're related to or otherwise associated with some celebrity who is often in the news, so they also get mentioned and photographed frequently. Some of these have tried to turn their fame into entertainment careers, but that comes after the fact; initially they were famous just for being famous.

Why do we care so much, as a society, about celebrities? Politicians' lives reveal their inward character, which gives us an idea of what kind of public servants they will be. But other celebrities' personal lives—actors, for example —don't affect how well they portray a character on screen for our entertainment. So why are we so interested? One answer might be because we see them so much on screen we feel as if we know them, so we are as interested as we would be with our friends. Another answer might be because we're told, indirectly but constantly, that celebrities' lives are worth our attention. Entire industries are built around this claim—magazines, paparazzi photos, TV talk shows, web shows, blogs. Entrepreneurs know that celebrity news brings in the money, so they dish up as much as they can. Many news programs have a "Hollywood Minute." Some might argue that media only gives us what we want; others say it generates the interest. Which came first—the chicken or the egg?

In this video -- www.ifyouonlynews.com/politics/texas-tech-students-give-jaw-droppingly-shocking-answers-political-questions-video/ -- college students who can't answer simple questions about US history and politics easily answer questions about celebrities. While this isn't as scientific as the studies mentioned above, it still reveals the pervasiveness of celebrity obsession in US culture.

An unhealthy level of interest in celebrities seems to have generated an unhealthy level of desire to become celebrities. Why do so many people, especially young people, want so badly to be famous? Maybe it's greed. The words "rich" and "famous" have gone together for decades, but that's far less true today than in the past. With YouTube, the 24 hours news cycle constantly needing fodder, and cameras in almost every pocket, anyone can become instantly famous without making a dime. Maybe the desire for fame comes from the appearance that celebrities get away with stuff. We often hear about a celebrity only getting a slap on the wrist for DUI or drug possession, which seems like unfair leniency simply because they're famous. An objective look at the facts doesn't support that misperception, but it is true that people with money and influence come through an arrest better than those who can't afford expensive lawyers. In fact, the opposite may be partially true: celebrities' mistakes are more talked about than those of normal folks. You probably wouldn't know it if your bank teller got a DUI, but you would hear about it if an actor from a show you watch did. Maybe the desire for fame comes from teens wanting attention. Sadly, most anyone who craves attention badly enough doesn't care whether the attention is positive or negative.

How we treat celebrities seems to cause some of them to think they are better than non-celebrities. A reporter for ESPN, Britt McHenry, was caught on video treating an impound lot attendant horribly, justifying her cruelty by saying, "I'm on TV." This is just one of many possible examples of how prideful celebrities think.

It's not talent that makes a celebrity. Nor skill. Nor beauty. Those things may help, but a person becomes a celebrity only by others paying attention to him or her.

THEOLOGICAL UNDERPINNINGS

As with many other topics, there is no Bible verse addressing whether celebrity is good or bad because no one was asking that question when the Bible was written. There are, however, verses that can guide our thinking on celebrity.

In Mark 7, Jesus includes pride in a list of things that defile a person. Pride, theologically speaking, is an exaggerated sense of one's own value and importance. Traditionally, pride is recognized as a sin. St. Augustine and many other theologians consider pride to be the sin that caused both Lucifer and Adam and Eve to fall.

Hebrews 11 mentions several people, some of whom had died thousands of years earlier, and all of whom we're still talking about another 2,000 years later. That's some enduring fame! Most of today's celebrities won't be remembered even 50 years from now. None of the people mentioned in Hebrews 11 set out to become famous. They were just being faithful to God and trying to serve the greater good. Millions more have done the same without any fame; we don't even know their names, but they received the same welcome in heaven.

In 1 Corinthians, Paul chastises Christians for dividing themselves based on which celebrity preacher they follow: Paul, Apollos or Cephas/Peter. He tells them to focus instead on following Christ.

In Galatians 2, Paul explains his own spiritual mindset , and challenges us to adopt it as well by saying, "I have been crucified with Christ; and it is no longer I who live, but it is Christ who lives in me." This mindset is the exact opposite of seeking fame for oneself. While Cumberland Presbyterianism doesn't say it's wrong to enjoy celebrities in movies and sports, or to want your own accomplishments to be recognized, we do believe Christians should strive to keep such things in their proper place. CP theology does affirm what the Bible says: everything starts with God. When we put God first, everything else is much more likely to fall into its proper and healthy place.

APPLYING THE LESSON TO YOUR OWN LIFE

Lacey Spears gained (in her mind, at least) "fame" for blogging about the difficulties of having a chronically ill child. It turned out she was poisoning him to achieve that fame, and eventually murdered her five-year-old. How do you react to stories such as this?

Do you think the internet and social media have made more people want to become famous, or just made fame seem easier to achieve?

If you are a consumer of celebrity news (personal information beyond concert dates, new releases, upcoming roles, etc.), would you be equally interested in the same details of other strangers' lives? Consider fasting from consuming celebrity news for a week or two and then assess how your spiritual life is affected.

How do you ensure that in your life, God comes first? How does your congregation teach members that God comes first? How do you practice humility? What opportunities does your congregation offer for members to practice humility?

JUST IN CASE

If any of your students seem to think being a celebrity would be wonderful, tell them about FKA Twigs (real name: Tahliah Barnett). She is a dancer-singer-songwriter in the UK who became the focus of celebrity news when she got engaged to mega-celebrity Robert Pattinson. About the attention paid to celebrities, she says, "It's really hard — I can't begin to explain how awful it is. It makes you want to just stop everything sometimes. It makes you want to smash your face into the mirror." Some of her song lyrics reflect this: "I wait all week for a moment's Break away from being told who I am," "We wait all week to hear gods talk when you've got a front-row seat to the stars." Neither her videos nor songs are appropriate for class.

WHAT MAKES A CELEBRITY?
BY JIMMY BYRD AND ANDY McCLUNG

SCRIPTURE
MARK 7:20-23, 1 CORINTHIANS 1:10-17, EXODUS 20:3-5A
HEBREWS 11: 4-7, 31-34, GALATIANS 2:19B-20A

⊙ LEADER PREP

- Newsprint or dry erase board
- Markers, paper, pens or pencils
- "American Idols" handout
- Set up a TV or laptop to watch http://www.ifyouonlynews.com/politics/texas-tech-students-give-jaw-droppingly-shocking-answers-political-questions-video/

BEFORE THE LESSON

Make sure you cue up the video clip listed in the LISTEN UP section to your phone, tablet, or computer. Make copies of the "American Idols" handout for each student.

⊙ GET STARTED
(5 minutes)

ASK: Have you ever met someone famous? Who was it? Where was it? Did you talk to the person, get an autograph, get a picture with them?

Were you nervous?

If you have time, follow up with these questions below, or use them in place of the previous questions.

ASK: If you could go out to eat with one celebrity for two hours, who would it be?

Why did you pick this celebrity? Where would you go eat and why?

⊙ LEADER INSIGHT
(20 minutes)

ASK: How many of you want to be famous someday?

SAY: It may be easier to be a celebrity today because of YouTube. Anyone can make their own videos and post them. Some videos go viral, meaning hundreds of thousands to millions of people see the video, and you can become a sensation overnight. There are also tons of reality shows on now that make everyday people celebrities on TV.

SAY: Imagine being a celebrity. Making tons of money and living the life! Depending on how famous you are, you may always be followed by photographers and reporters. People are always asking for your autograph or a picture. Sometimes you have to wear a disguise just so you can go about your business without being disturbed. Sometimes people stalk you and you have to get restraining orders against them. You get trashed on TMZ and other tabloids when you make a bad movie or make a mistake. What a life!

ASK: Did you know that even people in the Bible became obsessed with celebrities? Have someone read 1 Corinthians 1: 10-17. Paul is criticizing the people for following the celebrity of Apollos, Peter, and himself, instead of following Christ. Do we find Christians following their preachers more than following Christ today?

Do you remember the news story about Cecil the Lion? He was a beloved lion in Zimbabwe's Hwange National Park. He had become a local celebrity to the people there. He was killed in July 2015 by a trophy hunter. Overnight Cecil became an international celebrity. People were furious over his death. His death became a hot topic here in America and was featured on many national news outlets like CNN. Someone from Zimbabwe made a statement, though, that put things in perspective. He said he understood people's outrage over the death of Cecil the Lion, but where was that outrage over Zimbabwe's poverty, AIDS epidemic, and water shortages. This is an example of how we can get caught up in a celebrity obsessed story (in this case, a lion) and miss the big picture.

ASK: Why is our culture so obsessed with celebrities? What is it about them that takes so much of our attention?

Write down the answers on newsprint or dry erase board. Let students give several answers.

On a tablet, phone, or computer, show the following clip included in the background for this lesson. If you don't have internet in your classroom, you can try and save the video to your device ahead of time.

Show the clip:
http://www.ifyouonlynews.com/politicstexas-tech-students-give-jaw-droppingly-shocking-answers-political-questions-video/

SAY: Some people spend more time reading about their favorite celebrity than they do reading the Bible. Some know more about celebrity culture than they do their own culture. Some people know more about their favorite celebrity than they do about their own family!

ASK: What does this video say about us as a culture when it comes to celebrity obsession?

NOW WHAT?

(15 minutes)

SAY: The problem with our celebrity obsession is that it can become idol worship. In Exodus 20: 3-5a, it says, "you shall have no other gods before me. You shall not make for yourself an idol, whether in the form of anything that is in heaven above, or that is on the earth beneath, or that is in the water under the earth. You shall not bow down to them or worship them." (NRSV)

SAY: Whether we realize it or not, we have celebrity idol worship all around us. We even have a TV show called American Idol.

SAY: An idol or false god is anything that we give more attention to than God. We become more focused on the idol than we do with God.

Pass out the handout "American Idols," and give each student a few minutes to work on it. After everyone is finished, take time to go over their answers. Discuss why these idols have taken attention away from God.

Have someone read Mark 7: 20-23. In this passage, it mentions pride as an evil intention.

ASK: How can pride lead to us taking our focus off of worshiping God?

LIVE IT

(5 minutes)

SAY: In God's eyes, every one of you is important, you are a celebrity, but don't think too highly of yourself.

Read Galatians 2:19-20.

SAY: In this passage, Paul says that "it is no longer I who live, but is it Christ who lives in me." We are new creations because of Christ. Being filled with Christ should not make us prideful or arrogant. It should make us humble. To be important in God's eyes is a blessing. Go and be a blessing to others.

Close in prayer.

Resources used in compiling background information: jonathanmerritt.religionnews.com, news1130.com, nytimes.com, usatoday.com, teenadvice.about.com, Westminster Dictionary of Theological Terms, http://www. ifyouonlynews.com/politics/texas-tech-students-give-jaw-droppingly-shocking-answers-political-questions-video/ Pictures used: PAPARAZZI - http://i.huffpost.com/gen/942663/images/o-PAPARAZZI-facebook.jpg

American Idols

What are things that we are giving more attention to than God? These could be celebrities, but anything that distracts our focus from the one true God.

1. _____

2. _____

3. _____

4. _____

5. _____

6. _____

7. _____

8. _____

9. _____

10. _____

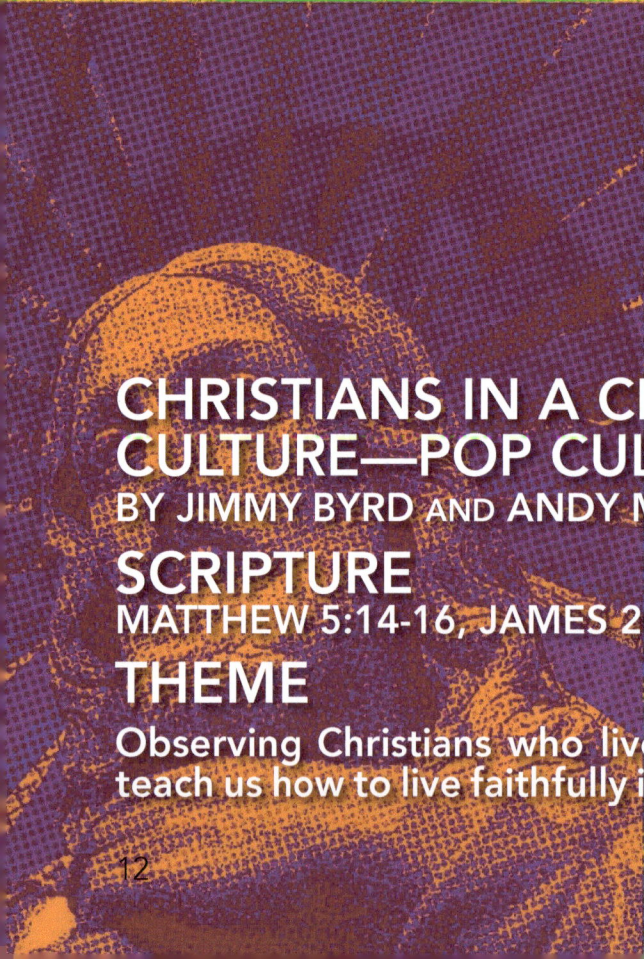

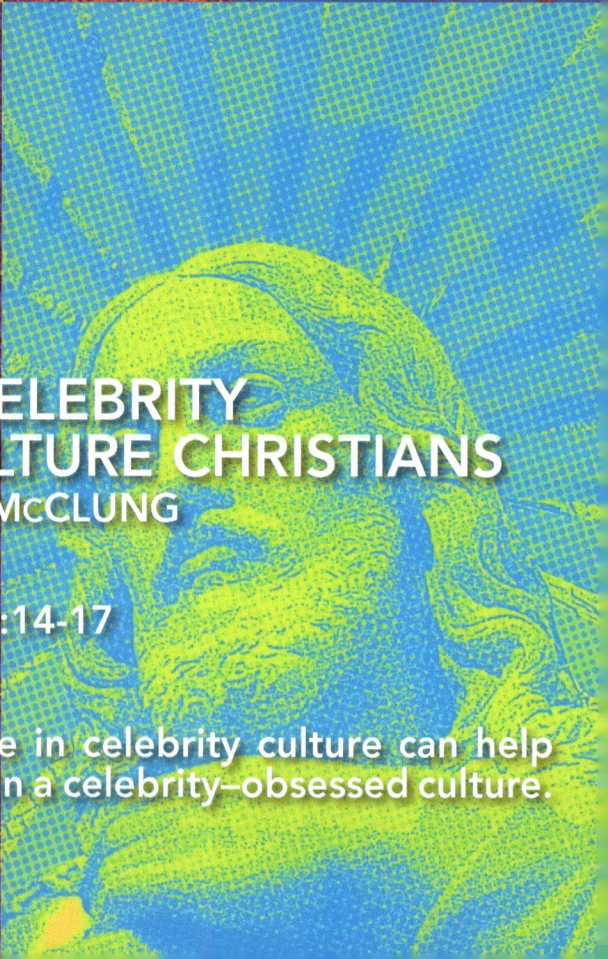

CHRISTIANS IN A CELEBRITY CULTURE—POP CULTURE CHRISTIANS

BY JIMMY BYRD AND ANDY McCLUNG

SCRIPTURE
MATTHEW 5:14-16, JAMES 2:14-17

THEME
Observing Christians who live in celebrity culture can help teach us how to live faithfully in a celebrity–obsessed culture.

ⓘLEADER INSIGHT

Your students probably don't care if the celebrities they like aren't Christian. Your students might, however, feel better about liking a particular celebrity if they heard them mention God, or if they saw a celebrity athlete make a religious motion (making the sign of the cross, kneeling as if in prayer, pointing to heaven, etc.). We should be careful, though, for such things do not necessarily mean someone is a Christian.

Some of your students may have experienced a situation in which they were—or would have been—embarrassed to express their own Christian beliefs and practices. Christian celebrities probably feel like this most of the time.

Taking a look at celebrities who may be Christian can help us in two ways. First, we can see how to keep one's faith in a non-Christian culture. Second, we can see how to tell the difference between true Christians and those simply acting the part.

EXPLAINING THE TOPIC

Celebrity extends beyond movies and TV, but we'll use "Hollywood" to refer to the celebrity culture in general.

Few celebrities are outspoken Christians, partially because Hollywood is run by many non-religious people. Ask an average American what percentage of the population regularly attends worship services, and they'll probably come close to the right answer of 40 to 60%. Ask Hollywood types, though, and you'll probably hear 5 to 20%. What is normal in Hollywood doesn't necessarily line up with the rest of society. Actress Brooke Burns said, "In L.A if you go to church you're crazy… when you bring it up, it becomes as controversial, if not more, than bringing up politics."

Here are some celebrities who claim to be Christian or who reportedly are Christian.

Bono, lead singer for the rock band U2 which has sold 140 million albums and won 22 Grammys, has stated very plainly that he attends church with his family, prays, and believes Jesus was the Son of God. His faith has led him to establish ONE, which fights poverty, AIDS, Tuberculosis, and Malaria in Africa.

Kristin Chenoweth is an actress on Broadway, in movies, and on TV. She's also a singer who has released both popular and Christian albums. She publicly and unashamedly claims to be a Christian.

Alice Cooper is a rock and roll legend. His band is in the Rock and Roll Hall of Fame. (Your students may know his song "School's Out.") He was the first rock star to incorporate horror-movie imagery into his act. Raised in a Christian home, he says he never stopped believing in Christ, but let alcohol turn him into "the poster boy for moral decay" for a while before he fully embraced his faith. Now he clearly and confidently talks about his Christianity. He says, "I'm the first one to rock as loud as I can, but when it comes to what I believe, I'm the first one to defend it." He openly shares the gospel with other musicians and holds an annual golf tournament which benefits at-risk youth through his charity, the Solid Rock Foundation.

Fergie, lead singer for the Black-Eyed Peas, and her movie star husband, Josh Duhamel, had a Catholic wedding and frequently attend Saturday night Mass together. She says it feeds their spiritual side, and she loves to hear her husband sing in church.

Matthew McConaughey is an actor who said, upon receiving an Oscar, "First off I want to thank God, because that's who I look up to. He's graced my life with opportunities that I know are not of my hand or any other human hand." He reportedly attends church when at home in Texas. He was in Time's 2014 list of the 100 most influential people. Chloe Grace Moretz is said to be a Christian by a few bloggers and the occasional comments of online fans. If so, she is not outspoken about it. She has publicly said that she grew up in a very traditional Christian family and did not cuss in her personal life, only in movies.

Martin Sheen is an actor and a Roman Catholic Christian whose real name is Ramon Estevez. He took the stage name "Sheen" from a Catholic theologian. He told an interviewer, "The essence of the Gospel of Jesus was extremely radical, and that's why they killed Him." Sheen believes his faith compels him to be politically outspoken, and he is.

Carrie Underwood is a singer in the country music industry, where it's less radical to be Christian than in other entertainment fields. She and her husband attend church (non-denominational), a weekly study group, have daily prayer time, and clearly confess to being Christians.

Denzel Washington is an A-List movie star who, in 2012, tied with Clint Eastwood for second place as America's favorite actor (Johnny Depp took first place). Washington says he's a Christian who reads the Bible and a devotional book every day. In an interview with GQ magazine, he talked about his experience of the Holy Spirit during a worship service decades ago at the church he still attends, a Church of God in Christ congregation.

At first glance, all of those folks seem legitimately Christian, and they very well may be. But carefully review those descriptions and you'll realize that some of these celebrities may not be Christians as we understand the term. Some perform in scanty outfits, simulate sex on camera, and do other things you won't find in your church. Some may recognize there is a God, but do not live as if Jesus is their Savior and Lord. This is not unfairly criticizing any of these celebrities, it's just pointing out that it's not always clear who is a Christian. When you look around at your church's membership, is it obvious who's really a Christian and who's just playing church?

THEOLOGICAL UNDERPINNINGS

Of the hundreds of Oscar acceptance speeches given over the last thirty years, only 14 people have thanked God. Some celebrities may be Christian, but keep their faith quiet because Hollywood isn't tolerant of some Christian beliefs. Still, some celebrities are openly Christian. And if they can worship and serve God through Christ while living and working in a culture that's not Christian, often intolerant of Christianity, and sometimes hostile toward Christianity, then so can we.

In Matthew 5:14-16, Jesus tells us not to hide our "light" under anything, but to let it shine where everybody can see it. Hiding your faith in Christ is preventing the light, or goodness, of Christ from reaching the world through you. Some Christian celebrities probably do this to protect their careers, but they shouldn't.

James 2:14-17 stresses that our Christianity should manifest itself in doing good things. Our Confession of Faith (6.06-6.09) says that being saved "produces the desire" to do acts of service, acts of mercy, and make moral choices that honor God, and that these good works are our grateful response to God's grace. Non-Christians can do good things without God's influence, but those acts bring glory to the person or to humanity in general. Good works done by Christians for Christ's sake bring glory to God.

Celebrities who talk about God but do no good works that glorify God, then, either aren't Christian or aren't living as Christ has called us to.

We're not to judge others (Matthew 7:1-2), but we must assess others' faith to know if they're worth emulating. Just because somebody goes to church and talks about God doesn't mean they're Christian. We should look for definitive evidence of Jesus Christ as Savior (they've accepted God's gift of forgiveness offered through Jesus) and Lord (they've made following Christ the most important thing in their lives). And we should be as definitive in our own words, actions, and lives, so anyone and everyone will be perfectly sure that we are Christians.

Applying the lesson to your own life
Recall the last few times you've seen a Christian portrayed as a character in a mainstream movie or TV show. Chances are that character was either crazy, clueless about real life, or turned out to be a hypocrite. Why is this so common?

Recall a time it was awkward or embarrassing—even dangerous—for you to reveal that you were a Christian, express your Christian beliefs, or for someone else to know that you go to church and read the Bible. How did you handle the situation? How do you feel about how you handled it? How do you think God feels about it?

Does it matter to you whether or not the celebrities you watch or listen to are Christian? Why or why not? Do you think it's hard to be a Christian and play roles or sing songs that glorify sinful behaviors? What about roles that negatively portray Christians? How do you think performers reconcile this?

DIGGING DEEPER

Some celebrities talk about being "spiritual," which sounds like something we might hear in church. But it isn't necessarily without other signs of faith. In an interview, actress Brooke Burns said, "I grew up in a Christian home. My spirituality has evolved into my own personal faith." That reflects where many celebrities end up spiritually; they take only what they like from Christianity, add whatever else they want from wherever they like (other religions, New Age thinking, pop psychology, self-help jargon), and end up with a custom-made religion. Doing this doesn't draw you closer to God, but actually pushes God aside to make you your own god. A huge part of Christianity is humbly submitting yourself to God, even accepting and obeying stuff we don't like or isn't comfortable. That doesn't happen when you pick and choose to make up your own religion.

A customized religion also sounds terribly lonely. Another big part of Christianity is community; we worship, fellowship, rejoice, sorrow, learn, grow, and serve together with fellow believers. Those things are impossible among people who are each practicing their own personal religions.

CHRISTIANS IN A CELEBRITY CULTURE— POP CULTURE CHRISTIANS
BY: JIMMY BYRD AND ANDY MCCLUNG
SCRIPTURE
MATTHEW 5:14-16, JAMES 2:14-17

LEADER PREP

- Dry erase board or newsprint
- Markers, pens, or pencils

BEFORE LESSON
Make sure you have space in your room for the activity in NOW WHAT?

GET STARTED
(5 minutes)

Have someone volunteer to pretend to have won an Oscar, a Grammy, or other prestigious award. (If you have more than one volunteer, that's OK.) If you have a trophy or some goofy object to present them with, that will make this even better. Let them give their acceptance speech to the rest of the class. Have them pretend the class is a huge crowd of Hollywood elite. Let them be as corny as they want while giving their speech (acting surprised, crying, etc). Take note if they thank God or Jesus in their speech.

LISTEN UP
(15 minutes)

On a dry erase board or a piece of newsprint, have your students list the current celebrities that they like. Give them a couple of minutes to make their list.

ASK: Now looking over this list, how many of these celebrities do you know to be a Christian? How important is it for you to know which celebrities are Christians and which are not?

Do you ever pay attention to whether or not a celebrity thanks God or Jesus when they win an award? Just because the celebrity thanks God or Jesus, does that make them a Christian?

How do you feel about a celebrity who thanks God for giving them the talent of acting but performs in a movie that is raunchy or explicit? What about a singer who thanks God for the ability to sing but uses lots of profanity in their lyrics?

Go over the list of "Christian celebrities" provided in the background information with your students.

ASK: Do any of the names on this list surprise you? Which ones?

Does claiming to be a Christian or identifying with Christians make you a Christian? Why or why not?

SAY: Some celebrities will say they are religious or spiritual but do not follow the teachings of Christianity. Some follow Scientology or Kabbalah or something they make up.

This could open up lots of questions about other religions. If you have a book on different religions, you might want to bring it to the lesson for reference, or you can always Google some of these religions too. There is also a former Faith Out Loud that tackles different religions.

ASK: What is the difference between being Christian and religious, and Christian and spiritual?

NOW WHAT?
(20 minutes)

SAY: The secular entertainment industry can be a difficult place for Christians to work in. Sometimes Christianity becomes Hollywood's punching bag in TV shows, movies, and by comedians. This is to say that sometimes Christians are portrayed as crazy, illogical, or outdated in the entertainment industry.

Divide the class into two groups. Give each group one of these passages of scripture: Matthew 5: 14-16 for group one, James 2: 14-17 for group two. After each group has gone over the scripture together, let them come up with a short skit or scenario based on the scripture. The skit needs to incorporate the meaning of the scripture passage. After each group performs, someone needs to read the scripture to the rest of the class.

SAY: Let's bring all this closer to home. Is it difficult for you as a Christian to let your light shine at school? At work? In the community? What makes it difficult?

ASK: What do these two passages of scripture say about how we are to live as Christians?

Why can't it always be easy like at church camp or on a youth retreat?

LIVE IT
(5 minutes)

SAY: In God's eyes every one of you is important; you are a celebrity. Remember that it may not always be easy to speak about your Christian faith, but it is important to live it. We all need to let our light shine, the light of Jesus Christ.

Resources used in compiling background information: foxnews.com, hollowverse.com, Hollywood vs. America by Michael Medved, jesusjournal.com, news.moviefone.com, one.org, publicreligion.org, theblaze.com, time.com.

SURRENDERING CELEBRITY FOR THE SAVIOR'S SAKE: GIVING IT UP FOR GOD
BY JIMMY BYRD AND ANDY McCLUNG

SCRIPTURE
MATTHEW 22: 36-39, 1 SAMUEL 7:3, 2 CORINTHIANS 5:17, 2 CORINTHIANS 6:14-16, EPHESIANS 4:29, EPHESIANS 5: 3-4

THEME
Following Christ always means giving up some things; for some celebrities, following Christ meant giving up fame and fortune

ⓘ LEADER INSIGHT

Some of your students may be on a team or group or club which stresses working for others over self-glorification. If so, good for them! The message from the world, however, is the exact opposite and much more common: look out for number one.

Following Christ is counter-cultural and counter-intuitive in that Christians are called to put God first, others second, and self-third. Celebrity culture is centered on putting self-first; getting noticed initially usually takes flagrant self-promotion, and established celebrities are surrounded by people treating them like the center of the universe.

There is also much in normal life to tempt us to the sin of pride, thinking and acting as if we're the most important thing there is. To help resist this temptation, we can learn something from those who gave up their celebrity status because they found it incompatible with their Christianity.

EXPLAINING THE TOPIC

Celebrity culture is obsessed with self, and some celebrities embrace just some parts of Christianity as if it's a feel-good, self-help program.

Celebrities who take their Christianity more seriously sometimes find they must leave that culture, either because they find the two lifestyles incompatible or because no one will hire them as outspoken Christians.

American culture as a whole is becoming less and less tolerant of Christianity, especially traditional or conservative Christianity. This isn't persecution, but Christianophobia. People lose jobs for stating what the Church and scripture have taught for millennia, particularly on homosexual activity. Abortion and church-and-state issues are also topics of contention. Catholic employers are forced to provide birth control coverage for their employees. Feeding the poor has become illegal in many cities. One city subpoenaed sermons of pastors opposed to a new city law dealing with homosexual and transgendered persons. Researcher George Yancey says this opposition isn't to Christianity in totality, but many people want Christians—particularly conservative Christians—to keep their religion completely private. Some Christian celebrities do this. But isn't that the exact opposite of what Christians are supposed to do?

There are several celebrities whose stories include addiction, not being able to get work, hitting rock bottom, and then becoming Christian. Some of them find work in the entertainment industry again, and some don't. But they're not our focus in this lesson. Listed here are some Christian celebrities who removed themselves from celebrity culture because they couldn't keep their faith private.

Kirk Cameron was a teen idol in the 1980s. As an atheist and celebrity, Cameron was convinced the world revolved around him. At 18 years old, he went to church to please a girlfriend, but the experience prompted him to start asking serious questions. Those questions eventually led him to accept Christ. He says he wanted to be who God created him to be, not who he wanted to be. Cameron learned to push self aside and allow Christ to be the lord of his life. His TV show, "Growing Pains," ended after seven seasons, partially because Cameron made too many demands trying to keep the show from violating his new morals. Cameron is still making movies, documentaries, and TV shows. The big difference is that all his work now is Christian-themed.

Angus T. Jones hit it big when he was cast on "Two and Half Men" and was the highest paid child actor for eight years. The show was #1 for years, and 18-year-old Jones was making $300,000 per episode, when a homemade video went viral. The video showed Jones calling the show "filth," saying he didn't want to be on it anymore and urging people not to watch it. Turns out, he had become a Christian a few months earlier. He couldn't continue living as what he called "a paid hypocrite," since the show glorified a sinful lifestyle. Jones has done nothing in Hollywood since his contract with CBS expired, and he doesn't want to. He has, however, studied the Bible and evangelism at his church. To any Christian wanting to become a celebrity, Jones says, "It is such a difficult thing to do without compromising your beliefs… You are either in the world or with God. Committing yourself to some kind of job that isn't committed to God is going to bring so much trouble into your life. It's not good and not something I would suggest that someone seek."

Montell Jordan isn't a familiar name, but his song "This is How We Do It" is. Jordan grew up in a Baptist church but ignored his upbringing to fit the image of a music celebrity. When his career suffered a setback, he turned back to his faith, fasting for 21 days and hearing God tell him to retire from R&B music. He did, and his new calling found him: making music that honors Christ. He is a worship leader and has organized a church band that performs concerts and makes recordings. He also records his own music, one of the few African-American performers in contemporary Christian music.

Chris Tucker started out as a stand-up comedian and became the highest paid actor in Hollywood (at the time) by earning $25 million for Rush Hour 3. He could easily have made several more movies for even bigger paychecks, but after making Money Talks, he became a Christian. He didn't leave stage and screen completely, but he did slow down drastically to focus on living life instead of making money.

Brian Welch, a famous guitarist, left the heavy metal band Korn, which he helped form. His decision came after becoming a Christian more than a year earlier and growing increasingly uncomfortable with the band's moral message. A weekend of prayer and Bible reading led him to the decision. He said he couldn't spend his life "chasing the almighty buck."

THEOLOGICAL UNDERPINNINGS

In Matthew 22:36-39, Jesus sums up all of God's rules for the right way to live by saying we should love God, others, and ourselves with everything we have… and in that order. To understand and live this commandment, some Christians, including celebrities, have to walk away from environments that pander to their every desire.

1 Samuel 7:3 tells the Israelites that following God means rejecting all the human-made gods they've experienced. Money and fame are human-made gods that some celebrities, and many other Christians, have rejected in order to follow the one true God.

2 Corinthians 5:17 says that those who accept salvation through Christ are new creations—in spirit and action. Even those of us raised in the Church should upon accepting Christ display some kind of positive change in behavior and attitude. For some, including some celebrities, this change involves leaving their career.

2 Corinthians 6:14-16a says that believers have to be careful about how closely they're connected to unbelievers. This doesn't prohibit having non-Christian friends or sharing Christ with others, but it does warn us to distinguish between believers and nonbelievers. Some celebrities, and many other Christians, have left their homes and livelihoods in order to keep themselves from being overly influenced by non-Christians.

Ephesians 4:29 and 5:3-4 speak about what we contribute to the world. Some actors and singers take this seriously enough to leave show business because roles or lyrics do not meet these criteria.

The Bible never says it's wrong to be rich, or to work hard to earn money, or to get paid for working. But 1 Timothy 6:9-11 does warn against both the desire to be rich and the love of money—two things which motivate many people to seek fame. People of God should instead pursue things such as righteousness, faith, and gentleness.

APPLYING THE LESSON TO YOUR OWN LIFE

Have you ever left a job/career for faith reasons? What fields could you not work in because of your faith? What would have to happen for your current place of employment to become a place where you, as a Christian, just couldn't work?

Is there more intolerance of Christianity in the news media, Hollywood, and the culture at-large recently? Is your answer verifiable and defendable, or just a perception? Is intolerance persecution, or simply non-believers acting like non-believers? Should Christians "fight back"? If so, what methods would be most Christ-like?

It seems that more conservative Christian celebrities leave "Hollywood" than liberal Christian celebrities. Why do you think this is?

Do you think it would be better to distance yourself from an environment that's intolerant of Christianity, or to stay in it so you can work for reconciliation from within? If your local municipality were to become intolerant of Christianity, would you stay or leave?

JUST IN CASE

No matter how meaningful the special worship services that happen inside the church are, the community outside the building can't see them. One way to share publicly the observance of Lent is to utilize an outdoor cross, even if it means erecting one specifically for Lent. A purple cloth can be draped on the cross throughout Lent, palm leaves can be affixed to it on Palm Sunday, the cloth switched to black on Good Friday, and then white on Easter Day. Plus, fresh flowers can be added to the palm leaves on Easter. One CP minister was once surprised to see a purple-draped cross outside a particular church building during Lent because it was of a non-liturgical denomination. The purple cloth stayed through Good Friday, Easter, and several months afterwards. Apparently they weren't being liturgical after all, but just thought it looked nice.

SURRENDERING CELEBRITY FOR THE SAVIOR'S SAKE: GIVING IT UP FOR GOD

BY JIMMY BYRD AND ANDY McCLUNG

SCRIPTURE

MATTHEW 22: 36-39, 1 SAMUEL 7:3, 2 CORINTHIANS 5:17, 2 CORINTHIANS 6:14-16, EPHESIANS 4:29, EPHESIANS 5: 3-4

LEADER PREP

- Video clip from God's Not Dead

https://www.youtube.com/watch?v=Qb2EZfeDMPU

- Blank paper for each student
- Pen or pencil for each student

BEFORE THE LESSON

Make sure you cue up the video from YouTube for the movie clip from God's Not Dead. The clip is called "GOD's not Dead - 1 John 4:4, who's greater?" It can be found at: https://www.youtube.com/watch?v=Qb2EZfeDMPU.

The clip can be found on DVD (if you already own the movie), but it is edited from different scenes. It will be easier to watch the YouTube clip if you can.

GET STARTED

(5 minutes)

SAY: Being a celebrity and a Christian is not always easy. Some celebrities feel the need to hide their faith, while others become so committed that they walk away from the celebrity lifestyle. Here are a few celebrities who have changed their celebrity lifestyles because of their faith in God.

Go over the list of celebrities in the background section of this lesson.

SAY: What do you think about the courage of these celebrities to stand up for their beliefs? What would you have done in their situation?

LISTEN UP

(15 minutes)

SAY: The movie God's Not Dead is about a student in college who refuses to sign a document for his Philosophy professor that says "God Is Dead." Because he won't do this, his professor challenges him to prove that God is not dead during debates in class, or face a zero for that section of the class.

Show the movie clip from the film "God's Not Dead."

SAY: Someone summarize what was happening in that scene.

ASK: Do you think Josh made the right decision? If you were in Josh's situation what would you do? Did the girlfriend have a point? Why or why not?

⊞ NOW WHAT?
(20 minutes)

No one said that following God would be easy. In fact, Jesus said quite the opposite. In order to fully commit ourselves to God, we usually have to give some things up. As you read in the beginning of this lesson, some celebrities have had to give up their Hollywood lifestyles in order to follow God's plan for their lives.

ASK: Have you had to give up something in order to follow God?

Give the students time to consider the question, and let any that feel comfortable share.

SAY: We are going to read over some different scripture passages on what it means to live according to God's plan and will.

If you have enough students, divide them up into pairs. Assign each pair one of the following scriptures:

- Matthew 22:36-39
- 1 Samuel 7:3
- 2 Corinthians 5:17
- 2 Corinthians 6:14-16
- Ephesians 4:29
- Ephesians 5:3-4

If you have a smaller class, you can assign one passage to each person or go through them as a group. Give each of the students a piece of paper and a writing utensil.

SAY: I want you to read over the scripture passage assigned to you. In five words or less, write down how this passage describes how we are to live our lives according to God's will.

Give students a few minutes to work on this. After all have finished, have them read the passage assigned and then read their five word statement.

SAY: Following God can be challenging. It causes us to live differently. God doesn't want us to live differently simply to seem weird or rebellious, but to live in a way that radiates God and promotes the message of Jesus Christ.

You can take the scripture passages and statements that the class have written and compile them onto one sheet of paper. Make copies of it, and give to the class at your next meeting. This could be a helpful reminder to the students to follow these teachings.
(5 minutes)

🌳 LIVE IT

SAY: In God's eyes every one of you is important—you are a celebrity. What are some things in your life that God is telling you to give up or to turn away from? What is holding you back?

Let the students think about these questions as you have a couple of minutes of silent prayer. After a couple of minutes, either you or one of the students close out the prayer.

Resources used in compiling background information: christianitytoday.com, imdb.com, laweekly.com, madamenoir.com, mtv.com, theblaze.com, time.com, https://www.youtube.com/watch?v=Qb2EZfeDMPU, God's Not Dead – 2013 – Pure Flix Entertainment Pictures used: Birds - https://goo.gl/d8r5vv

USING CELEBRITY FOR CHRIST
BY JIMMY BYRD AND ANDY MCCLUNG

SCRIPTURE
PSALM 1:1-3, MATTHEW 6:19-21, MARK 5:18-20,
ROMANS 12:4-8, EPHESIANS 4:10-12.

THEME
Christian celebrities can reach many people for Christ, reminding us that all Christians are called to use their platforms to share the gospel with others.

⚜LEADER INSIGHT

Your students may not consciously realize how much influence celebrities have, but they've seen the evidence. With a little guidance, they should be able to understand that celebrities affect lots of lives simply by what they choose to wear, drink, or drive; by what they say or how they wear their hair; and by what causes they support. People emulate celebrities.

Some of your students probably overestimate their influence over others. This may stem from being on a team or being popular. Some of your students probably underestimate their influence over others. This may stem from having low self-esteem or not being popular. Your students, then, may need help in gaining a realistic picture of how much potential influence they have over others. They probably can't get everybody in school to wear, let's say, a rainbow wig, but with a kind deed they can brighten someone's day and serve as a model for others to be kind as well.

EXPLAINING THE TOPIC

Cristal Champagne once had a huge market in young African-Americans because hip-hop artists featured it in their music videos. How many people once wore their hair like George Clooney (The Caesar) or Jennifer Anniston (The Rachel)? How many people bought a tiny dog after seeing Paris Hilton carrying one around? Nothing happened when non-celebrity Marcus Higgins tweeted what he thought was George Zimmerman's address (it wasn't), but when Spike Lee retweeted it there was a flood of threats against the residents there.

Celebrities have incredible influence in worldly matters. Celebrities who are outspoken Christians -- whether they like it or not, whether they deserve it or not – have truly significant influence in the lives of other Christians and represent Christianity to nonbelievers.

Stephen Baldwin wasn't a huge star, but he's still a celebrity. His Hollywood career suffered when he became an outspoken Christian, but he used his celebrity status to become a speaker for different teen ministries. He even started a ministry to reach teens through skateboarding.

Former US president Jimmy Carter is a political celebrity. Most presidential candidates have claimed to be Christian, but Carter visibly lived as a Christian. This hurt him in office, but has helped him since. After leaving office, he established the Carter Center, worked with Habitat for Humanity, and is part of an independent group of influential persons from around the globe who work together for peace and human rights, known as the Elders.

Bethany Hamilton was a surfer who, at the age of 13, became a celebrity in the worst way possible: by losing an arm in a shark attack. Her faith helped her recover. She was already a Christian, but her celebrity status allowed her to speak of her faith in interviews, publish a book, have a movie made about her, and establish Friends of Bethany, a charity which encourages "amputees and youth by offering hope to overcome through Jesus Christ."

Dean Koontz is as much of a celebrity as a novelist who avoids publicity can be. Forty-five of his novels have been on the New York Times' bestseller list. Koontz's novels are full of violence and good vs. evil. He says he writes about "our struggle as fallen souls, about the grace of God." His Christianity sneaks in too, but not so in-your-face that it's going to run off non-Christians. His writing has planted seeds of curiosity about the mystery of God in millions of readers, seeds waiting to be nourished.

Tom Landry was more than a celebrity; he's a legend. He coached the Dallas Cowboys to 20 consecutive winning seasons. After winning Super Bowl VI in 1972, his was a household name. Everybody knew he was a good coach, and anybody who paid attention knew he was a Christian. Landry was a member of a Methodist church for decades, even teaching an adult Sunday school class while coaching. It's said he'd arrive for Sunday afternoon home games at the last minute because of teaching. A posthumous biographer called him "a fiercely Christian man" who kept his moral compass during a time when the country was in moral chaos. Tons of people interested in football have heard about Jesus through Landry's interviews, biographies, and autobiography.

Tyler Perry says there are other Christian filmmakers who keep their faith in the closet, but he's not afraid to have characters talk about their faith. (Madea, his most famous character, does not.) He's not preachy in his work, though. He says, "While making people laugh, I can drop in pearls of wisdom. That's like tilling the soil for the seeds to be planted. And that's what I've tried to do, to plant seeds that will grow into… abundant life for many people."

Deion Sanders is the only professional athlete to hit a home run and score a touchdown in the same week, and the only person to play in both the Super Bowl and the World Series. At the height of his career he realized that all the power, money, and sex that fame had brought him didn't fill the void within him. But he found what did: a relationship with God through Jesus Christ. He is vocal about his faith, speaking about it in interviews and publishing an autobiography.

Celebrities who are outspoken Christians face a particular danger: because they're celebrities, they're paid a lot of attention; but because they're human, they sin. When lots of people are watching you sin, those sins seem magnified. (Mel Gibson is a Christian, but his drunk driving arrest is legendary.) Some Christians seem to lose all faith in a Christian celebrity whose sins are exposed, when we really should treat them just as we do any other fellow believer who sins; which, hopefully, is with forgiveness and encouragement. In other words, we should treat them as God treats us when we sin.

THEOLOGICAL UNDERPINNINGS

Celebrities have lots of resources – both human and financial – to do what they need to get done. What Christian celebrities need to get done is sharing their faith with others and doing good works… just like every believer. Christian celebrities automatically have an audience, people listening to what they say and watching what they do. If they're willing to be open about their faith this makes sharing Christ and doing good works easier for them than us non-celebrities. When any of us normal people do an inventory, however, we can probably compile quite a list of gifts, skills, knowledge, opportunities, and contacts that we can use to serve God and represent Christ.

In Mark 5:18-20, Jesus tells a man recently freed from a demon to tell others about Jesus. Whenever we are freed from sin or our personal demons by Jesus, we ought to do the same. The freed man was well known in the area and therefore had ready-made audience. Each of us already has an audience of family, friends, and acquaintances.

Psalm 1:1-3 can help us to keep our moral compass straight in a sinful and chaotic world. When we do, we yield "fruit" (results, good things) for God.

Romans 12:6-7 and Ephesians 4:11-12 teach that we each have God-given gifts. These gifts are not exhaustive. God can and does make gifts out of everything from writing music to being in a certain place at a certain time, and expects believers to use these for God's glory.

An entire section (6.00) of our Confession of Faith is entitled "Christians Live and Witness in the World." Witnessing isn't optional, even if we treat it that way, and we're able to do it in many ways: telling others what Jesus did for us, acts of service and mercy, making moral choices, using money and natural resources well (Confession 6.01-6.14).

APPLYING THE LESSON TO YOUR OWN LIFE

Imagine that you become a celebrity. Do you think you would be outspoken about your faith, even though you're pretty sure it will limit your earning potential, or will you keep quiet about your faith so you'll be more successful in your career?

How outspoken about your faith are you in your current vocation?

What gets more attention from the media, when Christian celebrities do good things (such as starting a charity), or when Christian celebrities say something about their faith that some might consider controversial? Why do think this is?

Do an inventory of your potential audience: in a typical month, how many different people do you have some kind of contact with? How many of those contacts do you somehow use to spread the gospel by witnessing, inviting people to church, doing works of service or mercy (just being nice doesn't count). Consider trying to double that number in the coming month.

JUST IN CASE

If your students are more oriented toward sports than Hollywood, consider mentioning some of the following outspoken Christians. Allyson Felix, Olympic runner and gold medal winner, credits God for her incredible speed. She readily says she accepted Christ at six years old and prays and reads the Bible daily. Derek Fisher, professional basketball player, has functioned as the unofficial chaplain for every team he's played on. Jake Peavey, baseball pitcher, was arrested in Dominican Republic for a traffic violation. He was there to introduce poor children to baseball and Jesus. He took the opportunity to share Christ with the police, jailers, and other prisoners. Michael Waltrip, NASCAR driver, talks about his faith in interviews. He also works with Motor Racing Outreach, which shares Christ with NASCAR drivers, crews, and their families. Encourage your student athletes to participate in, or start, FCA (Fellowship of Christian Athletes). Also, you may want to check out athletesinaction.org, a ministry supported by many professional athletes.

USING CELEBRITY FOR CHRIST
BY JIMMY BYRD AND ANDY MCCLUNG
SCRIPTURE
PSALM 1:1-3, MATTHEW 6:19-21, MARK 5:18-20, ROMANS 12:4-8, EPHESIANS 4:10-12.

LEADER PREP

- Copies of the handout "I Am a Celebrity in God's Eyes"
- Bibles
- Pens or pencils for each student
- Cell phone or tablet if you want to film the commercial in LISTEN UP
- Youtube clip: https://www.youtube.com/watch?v=l-gQLqv9f4o

BEFORE THE LESSON
Make copies of "I Am a Celebrity in God's Eyes" handout for each student. Cue up the YouTube video of Kid President for LIVE section. You can use a phone, tablet, or computer to show it. If you do not have an internet connection you can download the video before class to your device.

GET STARTED

(5 minutes)

ASK: Have you ever bought something simply because one of your favorite celebrities had endorsed it? (this could be shoes, clothes, deodorant, head phones, etc)

Have you ever gone to a concert and noticed people that dressed like the performers on stage? (ripped jeans and t shirts for rock concerts, cowboy hats and boots for country, Hawaiian shirts for Jimmy Buffett)

Have you ever gone to a ballgame and seen people wear jerseys of their favorite players?

SAY: While there is nothing wrong with doing any of these things, isn't it amazing how someone famous can influence you?

Nike signed Lebron James to a contract right out of high school. The contract, to use his celebrity status to sell shoes, was for $90 million dollars. (Kurt Badenhausen - Forbes Magazine, March 18, 2015.)

🎧 LISTEN UP
(20 minutes)

Have a student or students make a commercial. In this commercial they will pretend to be their favorite celebrity or celebrities. Have them use their celebrity status to sell their product. The commercial must be 30 seconds or less and they can either perform for the class or film on a phone or tablet and then play it back like on TV.

SAY: Not all celebrities use their influence to sell products. Some celebrities use their influence for charitable organizations and to bring awareness to some injustices in the world.

SAY: Some celebrities who are outspoken Christians use their status to promote their faith and values.

(Look at the information at the beginning of this lesson that features several Christian celebrities and how they use their influence to represent their faith. Read over this with your students.)

ASK: Which is most important, for celebrities to use their status for their own personal gain or for the promotion of the kingdom of heaven?

Have someone read Matthew 6:19-21.

When it comes to advertising and teens, it's astonishing the great lengths that corporations will go to target them. Several years ago there was a special on PBS called "The Merchants of Cool." This was an episode in their Frontline series. This show focused on how teens were being studied to help in their marketing strategy. This was a very interesting show on how our teens are being used by MTV and others to make the next big commercial success. You can find it on PBS.org.

🌐 NOW WHAT?
(15 minutes)

Have someone read Psalm 1: 1-3

ASK: So what about us? Normal, everyday people, everyday Christians, what can we do to promote Christianity? How can we use our talents and abilities to showcase God's love and power?

Who are some everyday people you know or have seen carry out things like this?

Give each student a copy of "I Am a Celebrity in God's Eyes". Have them take time to read it over and fill it out. After everyone has finished, give them time to share their answers and ideas.

🌳LIVE IT
(5 minutes)

Show this YouTube video clip from Kid President:
https://www.youtube.com/watch?v=l-gQLqv9f4o

SAY: In God's eyes every one of you is important, you are a celebrity. Think about the different ways that God has called YOU to serve and proclaim.

Give everyone a couple of minutes of silent prayer to talk to God about what they can do to serve God better. After a couple of minutes, close the session in prayer.

Resources used in compiling background information: amazon.com, beliefnet.com, bethanyhamilton.com, christianitytoday.com, imdb.com, ncregister.com, theelders.org, thesmokinggun.com , "Lebron James is NBS's Top Shoe Salesman With $340 Million For Nike" Kurt Badenhausen - Forbes Magazine, March 18, 2015, "Frontline – Merchants of Cool" – PBS.org, https://www.youtube.com/watch?v=l-gQLqv9f4o

I am a Celebrity in God's Eyes

As a child of God, you are important!

God wants to work through you

to reach others and

spread the good news of Jesus Christ.

You have been given talents and gifts

from God to use and carry out.

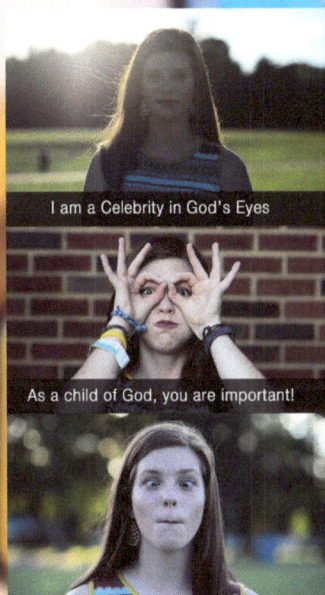

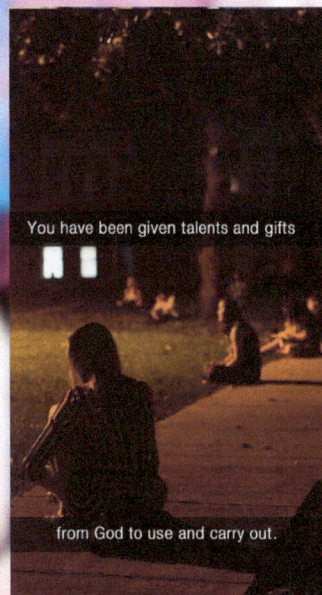

Read the following scripture passages:

- Romans 12:4-8 & Ephesians 4:10-12

How can you use your status as a follower of Christ to share the Gospel and promote Christ? As you have read above, you are equipped with gifts and abilities.

1) What activities are you involved in? (clubs, organizations, sports, etc.)

2) What leadership positions do you hold in school, in work, in church, etc.?

3) What things are you good at? (art, writing, sports, computers, listening, etc.)

4) What are you passionate about? (feeding the hungry, stopping slavery, providing clean water, providing clothing, stopping bullying, etc.)

Now, how can you make a difference? Look over your answers, and see how you can use those answers to glorify God. You are indeed a celebrity in God's eyes because you are God's creation!

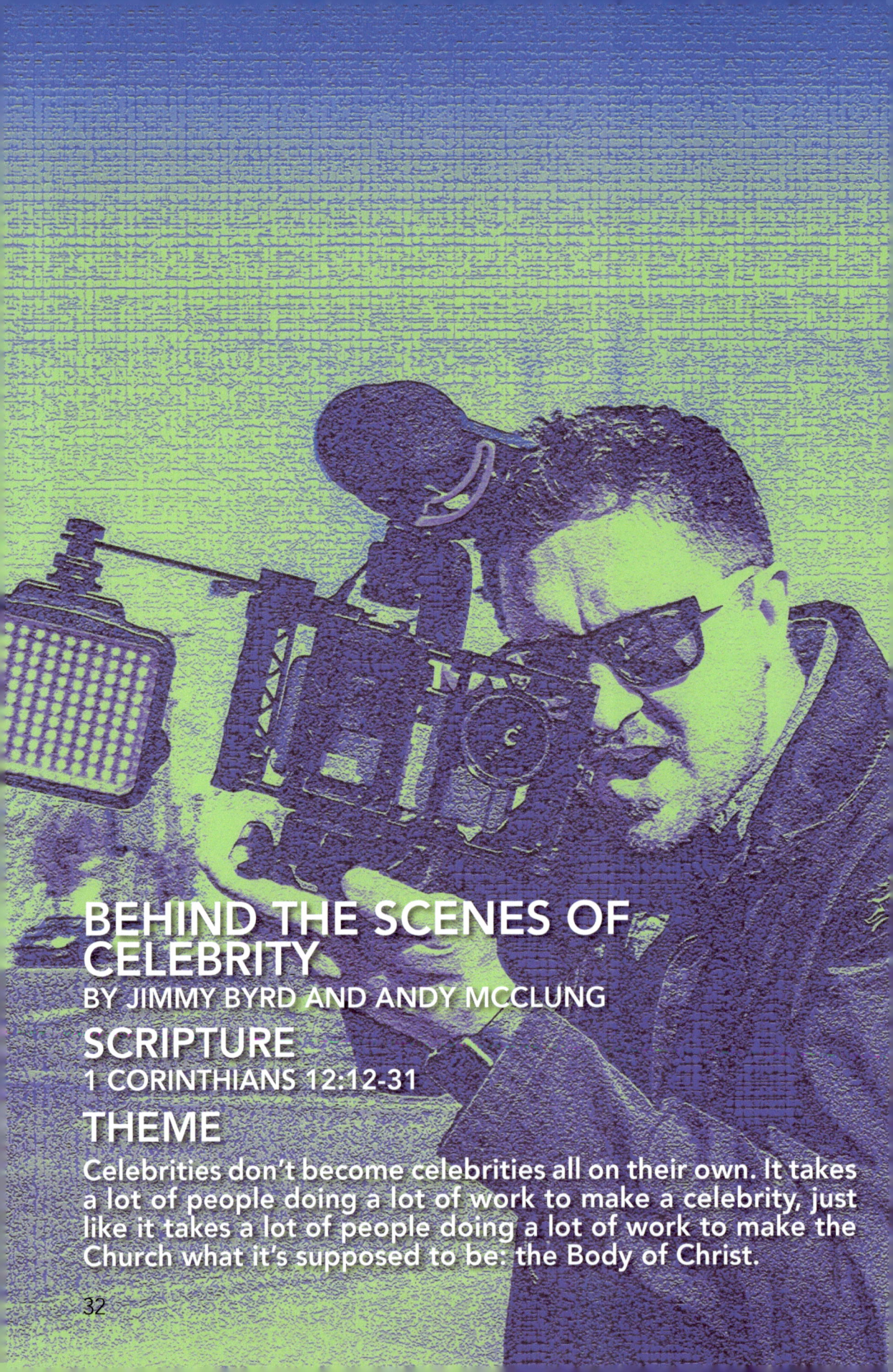

BEHIND THE SCENES OF CELEBRITY

BY JIMMY BYRD AND ANDY MCCLUNG

SCRIPTURE
1 CORINTHIANS 12:12-31

THEME
Celebrities don't become celebrities all on their own. It takes a lot of people doing a lot of work to make a celebrity, just like it takes a lot of people doing a lot of work to make the Church what it's supposed to be: the Body of Christ.

🪙 LEADER INSIGHT

When Josh Hutcherson appears on the movie screen or Ariana Grande starts singing, all eyes are on them. But it takes a lot a lot of people to get and keep them there.

Everybody notices the drum major, standing alone, but not the third trumpet. Everybody cheers when the batter hits a line drive just inside the third-base foul line, but nobody notices how straight somebody chalked that foul line. Some of your students may know how it feels to work "behind the scenes" and get little or no credit for it.

Some of your students may prefer to work on the sidelines or behind the curtain, but some of them may long for recognition. Some people who work behind the scenes really want to become celebrities and are simply trying to stay close to the action in the hope that they'll beat the odds and be discovered. Others are content to be a small part of a large industry and let someone else get all the attention.

EXPLAINING THE TOPIC

A celebrity quarterback can't pass the football downfield without linemen protecting him. A celebrity track star had coaches and teammates helping her train for years. Nobody becomes or remains a celebrity without lots of help from others. Since we can't cover every celebrity-making field, let's look at just some of the people it takes to put a celebrity on the screen of your local cinema.

Executive producers are the driving force behind a movie and have the final word on everything. They initiate the whole thing and take care of business stuff like finding investors, securing facilities, choosing the marketing and distribution companies, as well as hiring the producer, the director, and the writer.

Every movie starts as a script. Either a writer sells a completed script to an executive producer, or an executive producer comes up with an idea for a movie and hires a writer to write a script. Other writers sometimes do partial re-writes along the way.

Producers take care of day-to-day business decisions while the movie is being made, including watching the budget. They may also help cast the actors.

The director guides both the actors and the technical crew (camera operators, special effects, lighting, set design, etc.) toward the director's artistic vision of what the movie is about. Some movies also have a second unit director who's in charge of filming scenes like crowds, scenery, objects, etc.

The casting director chooses the actors for speaking roles, usually with some input from the producer and director.

The production designer creates the overall visual appearance of a movie. The costume designer creates each character's costume to fit that appearance. Extras are actors in crowd scenes. There are camera operators, lighting technicians, and electricians. There are people who design, build, and paint the sets. There are location scouts, and caterers. Production accountants make sure everybody gets paid. Production assistants do anything they're asked. Stunt coordinators design stunts and supervise stunt performers. Plus, there are editors, computer animators, dance choreographers, musicians, and tons of other people needed to make a movie.

All these people have to do their individual parts and also work together to make the movie. If they don't do their jobs, the movie doesn't get made and the celebrities don't get put before the public, which means they may not remain celebrities.

Presumably, there are some Christians working behind the scenes in Hollywood as caterers, extras, electricians, tutors for child actors, etc. There are definitely some Christians working behind the scenes in mainstream Hollywood movies who have more prominent positions.

Philip Anschutz is the 104th richest person in the world (worth $12.4 billion). Among other things, he runs Walden Media and has produced the Chronicles of Narnia movies, Nim's Island, Journey to the Center of the Earth (2008), Holes, and other family-friendly movies. Already rich, he got into movie making when he became disappointed that there weren't more movies appropriate for his grandchildren to watch.

Scott Derrickson is a writer, director, and producer who has mainly worked in horror movies like The Exorcism of Emily Rose. He says horror "is a perfect genre for Christians to be involved with. [It] deals… with the supernatural… it distinguishes and articulates the essence of good and evil better than any other genre. The genre is not about making you feel good, it is about making you face your fears. And in my experience, that's something that a lot of Christians don't want to do."

Barbara Hall has written episodes of Joan of Arcadia, Homeland, Northern Exposure, other TV series. She created the show Madame Secretary and was executive producer of Joan of Arcadia. She has received three Emmy nominations.

Howard Kazanjian was executive producer of Raiders of the Lost Ark and producer of Return of the Jedi, two of the biggest money-making movies ever. Outside of producing and directing, he serves on the board of a Christian college in California.

Andrea Nasfell wrote Mom's Night Out. She co-owns an independent film and TV production company.

Ralph Winter produced the first several X-Men movies and lots of others. He says he looks for movies with spiritual themes. When asked how he maintains his faith, he credits the "support system" he has in his wife and a few close friends who keep him spiritually accountable. He also teaches at Christian conferences and produces smaller budgeted, Christian-themed movies. He says, "I have been placed in this job for a purpose, and I am just trying to make great movies and keep my eyes on [God]… It is definitely all God's hand that I get to do this."

Tom Shadyac directs and produces mostly comedies, including Bruce Almighty and Evan Almighty. When criticized for working on a movie that portrayed the protagonist engaging in sinful behavior, he brought up St. Augustine's sordid life as recounted in his Confessions and the fact that St. Paul killed Christians before becoming one himself. He says, "You can't have the end of the story without the beginning of the story." Part of the story is how knowing God changes our behavior.

THEOLOGICAL UNDERPINNINGS

John Donne wrote "No [one] is an Island Entire of Itself." Donne was probably speaking about life in general, but he may also have meant being part of the Church. He definitely was not talking about being a celebrity in 21st Century America, but his words are applicable there as well.

In Genesis 1:26-27, God created humankind as a group, male and female in community, just as he'd done with all other living things. In the gospels, we see Jesus serving as rabbi to a group of disciples, not individuals. In the epistles, the Church is referred to as the Body of Christ. In the Cumberland Presbyterian Constitution, it's clear that each Christian is part of a congregation, each congregation is part of a presbytery, each presbytery is part of a synod and the General Assembly, and our whole denomination is a part of the Church Universal.

What might happen if we consider Jesus the celebrity and ourselves as each having some small, behind-the-scenes job to do in order to put Jesus out there for the world to see and adore? In the first lesson in this series, we said the only thing that can make someone a celebrity is people paying attention to him or her. Jesus is Messiah and Savior whether or not anybody pays attention to him, but for anybody to welcome Jesus into their lives, they have to pay attention to him. It's the church's job to promote him in such a way that people will want to do so.

Accepting Jesus is a decision each person has to make for him or herself. But usually when someone does make that decision, it's the result of a lot of people having done a lot of different things—parents, Sunday school teachers, youth leaders, pastors, elders all have a hand. And it takes these same people doing even more for that person to grow from a believer into a disciple.

APPLYING THE LESSON TO YOUR OWN LIFE

When have you been a small part of something big? Did you want a bigger role?

Next time you go to the cinema or watch a DVD, try to count the names in the end credits. Do you think each of them watches the completed movie with a sense of accomplishment?

Which position would you be best at: writer, director, producer, costume designer, etc.? Why do you think some people take on multiple positions in making a movie (writing, directing, and producing, for example)?

Many Christian movies seem to have low production values (acting, directing, etc.). If you agree, why do think this is so? Can a good message make up for a poorly made movie?

According to a seven-year study by Movie Guide, Hollywood movies portraying good morals and traditional Judeo-Christian values make lots more money than movies featuring atheist or anti-Christian values and immorality. If this study is accurate, why aren't there more of the former?

How does your congregation emphasize that each Christian, and each congregation, and each denomination is part of something bigger?

JUST IN CASE

If any of your students feel called to careers in the entertainment industry, consider pointing them to actoneprogram.com. Act One's mission is "to create a community of Christian professionals for the entertainment industry who are committed to artistry, professionalism, meaning, and prayer, so that through their lives and work they may be witnesses of Christ and the Truth to their fellow artists and to the global culture."

BEHIND THE SCENES OF CELEBRITY
BY JIMMY BYRD AND ANDY MCCLUNG

SCRIPTURE
1 CORINTHIANS 12:12-31

🌟LEADER INSIGHT

- Dry erase board or newsprint
- Markers
- Movie clip featuring just credits
- Youtube clip https://www.youtube.com/watch?v=foJ2eT0BwZQ
- One puzzle of at least 30 pieces or create your own puzzle but cutting up the front of a cereal box or make copies and enlarge the puzzle at the end of this lesson.

BEFORE THE LESSON

Make sure you cue up the YouTube video on a device. If you do not have the internet, you can download it ahead of time. When you have the students work on the puzzle, you need to remove one piece so that the puzzle is not complete. This is an object lesson to show the importance of every piece working together.

GET STARTED (5 minutes)

ASK: How many of you want to be famous someday?

What do you want to be famous for? (actor, actress, author, singer, inventor, musician, etc.)

Give students a chance to share their answers.

On newsprint or dry erase board, make a list of the most popular celebrities today.

ASK: How many of the people on this list do you think needed help to get famous?

Who do you think helped them?

Can you get famous on your own, or will you need help to get there?

🎧LISTEN UP

(20 minutes)

Ask your students to name all the different jobs titles for people that work on movies or TV shows. For example, in addition to the actors and directors, there are producers, make-up artists, set designers, script writers, etc.

Write down all the different job titles on a piece of newsprint or dry erase board.

SAY: It takes a lot of work behind the scenes to make Tom Hanks a household name or to make Taylor Swift America's sweetheart.

You can also show the credits to a movie. Be sure it is a movie where there are no interruptions during the credits. By watching the credits, the students can see all the many different jobs that go into making a movie.

ASK: If you have been to a concert, what are some of the jobs behind the scenes there? Write down the answers.

SAY: As we can see, it takes many people behind the scenes to make celebrities look good.

What about behind the scenes at church? The purpose of church is not to make the pastor or the choir look good. The purpose of church is not even to make God look good. God is already good; we don't have to make God look good. We are to worship and celebrate God's goodness and love. Our worship and living a life devoted to God enhances God's glory.

ASK: To showcase God's goodness and love, what goes on behind the scenes at church? What goes into making a church work the way it is supposed to?

Give students time to think over the answers to this. Allow a few minutes for discussion.

Show students this two minute YouTube video clip. It is a commercial from Honda that shows how many parts make up one vehicle. All of the parts in the commercial are Honda parts from the car. https://www.youtube.com/watch?v=foJ2eT0BwZQ

Read 1 Corinthians 12:12-31

ASK: What does this passage have to do with our role behind the scenes in church?

With the video and this scripture in mind, how important is each individual car part to the car or each individual person to the church?

⊞ NOW WHAT?
(15 minutes)

Tell the group that they are going to work on a puzzle together. Take the puzzle out of the box, and dump it on a table. Give students time to work on the puzzle. Don't say anything about there being a missing piece. Let the students figure it out as they complete it.

Once students have finished the puzzle, give them a chance to search for the missing piece. Of course they won't find the missing piece because you have left it out on purpose.

ASK: So is it complete? How frustrating is it to come this far and have the last piece missing?

SAY: Just like each individual piece makes up this puzzle, each of you make up the church. You are each important to the ministry here.

ASK: How important is it for everyone to do their role in the church?

What is your role at this church, or have you ever thought about that?

What is your role in promoting the goodness and love of God?

In the Faith Out Loud series on super heroes, there is a lesson on teamwork and your role in the church. There is a link to a basic spiritual gifts inventory that you can give to your students. If your students have not already taken this spiritual gifts inventory, have them fill it out. Here is the link: http://www.teensundayschool.com/122/activities/spiritual-gifts-analysis.php

🪙 LEADER INSIGHT

(5 minutes)

Give each student a piece of the puzzle, or let them choose which piece they want. This is to remind them that they are important to the ministry of the church. It takes every piece working together.

SAY: In God's eyes, every one of you is important—you are a celebrity. Think about how each of you can work together to promote the body of Christ in our community and to our world.

Close in prayer.

Resources used in compiling background information: beliefnet.com, christianitytoday.com, forbes.com, hollywoodjesus.com, imdb.com, movieguide.com, moviestaff.com Pictures used: NeONBRAND on Unsplash.com, Photo by Hans-Peter Gauster on Unsplash.com

FAITH OUT LOUD

ABOUT THE AUTHORS

Andy McClung, a lifelong Cumberland Presbyterian, was ordained to the ministry of word and sacrament in 1995. He earned a Master of Divinity and Doctor of Ministry from Memphis Theological Seminary and has served churches in Alabama, Mississippi, Tennessee, and Arkansas. He now enjoys serving the CP Church on the presbytery, synod, and denominational levels. Andy lives in Memphis, Tennessee with his wife (also a CP minister) and their two children.

Jimmy Byrd is the pastor of New Hope Cumberland Presbyterian Church in Whitwell, Tennessee. He is married to Jennifer and has two sons, Daniel and Matthew. Jimmy has served in youth ministry for over 20 years in the Cumberland Presbyterian Church. He is a graduate of Bethel University and received his Master of Divinity at Memphis Theological Seminary.